AF406073

The Influence of French Phonetics on Vocal Technique in French Art

Nyiko Condry Ngobeni

Title: **The Influence of French Phonetics on Vocal Technique in French Art**

ISBN: 979-8-89248-960-7

Author: Nyiko Condry Ngobeni

Cover image: https://pixabay.com/

Publisher: Generis Publishing
Online orders: www.generis-publishing.com
Contact email: info@generis-publishing.com

The Influence of French Phonetics on Vocal Technique in French Art

Nyiko Condry Ngobeni

Walter Sisulu University, Mthatha, Eastern Cape, South Africa,5100

nngobeni@wsu.ac.za

Abstract

This study focuses on French phonetics in vocal performance and its relationship to interpreting French art songs. It explores how the French vowels and consonants affect articulation, resonance and emotional expression. The research explores the connection between how we pronounce and how that changes a voice, both in how correct the consonant sounds can be and how that builds and supports how resonant, full and clear our sound is. The dynamics the singer can produce in performance. The paper also delves into the historical development of French phonetics and how it affects the reading of French vocal works, arguing for the significance of knowing historical phonetic changes to perform authentically. The review further discusses pedagogical techniques for teaching French phonics, blending traditional modes with more contemporary technological tools, including interactive software and online content. This research recommended that it is important to approach singing French phonetics flexibly and holistically to help singers perform French art songs linguistically and artistically. Finally, the review reflects on broader implications for vocal pedagogy, specifically concerning multilingual singers. It encourages further investigation into how phonetic challenges in French compare to those in other languages.

Keywords: French phonetics, Vocal technique, Articulation, Nasalization, Comparative analysis

Contents

Introduction

Mélodies, or French art songs, are rooted in the 19th century when France went through an era of artistic and cultural rejuvenation with the equilibrium of text and music being in perfection. This genre is characterised by its spare text setting, making extreme demands on singers for vocal technique and linguistic precision. Moreover, with texts often drawn from the works of well-known poets, including Victor Hugo, Paul Verlaine and Charles Baudelaire, with scores by Gabriel Fauré, Claude Debussy and Henri Duparc, the mélodie also requires performers to find that elusive balance between phonetic precision and interpretative freedom. These demands thus elevate French art songs to the levels of the classical repertoire for which mastery of the spoken word and the expression of the music are inextricably intertwined (Macy, 2008).

The peculiar phonetic reality of the French language is at the core of these works. Other than many other dialects, french has an intricate vowel system (closed ([i]) and open ([ɑ]) vowels, nasalised sounds, and little consonantal sound differentiation of voiced/unvoiced pair). This guarantees the text to be understood and works for a more emotional or expressive music setting. Vowels like those in bien and sans have nasal quality in French, so singers must be careful how they do this. Nasalisation, emitting from the mouth and nose, risks blurring the colour of the vowels and integrity of the language for singers. The consonants, though they take a back seat to the vowels in singing, are sonic forces. When done poorly, they can interfere with the flow of the musical line and emotional effect. The phonetic or phonological details are essential to creating the aesthetics and communicative potential of the performance itself (Bernac, 1967, as paraphrased in Machaney, 2006).

Though artistically rewarding, mélodies pose unique difficulties, particularly for non-native speakers. Mispronunciation or wrong vowelisation in a vocal utterance can shatter not just the linguistic legibility but also the visceral communicability of the performance. The French language is so delicate, so nuanced in its phonetic twists and turns and prolonged phrasing that one misplaced phoneme can throw off the balance. Moreover, the genre's texts can be poetic, limiting singers to a life of proper interpretation, which fundamentally needs a readiness to explore each piece's historical, literary and emotional depth. This duality of language highlights the need for performers to be educated in French phonetics and how to balance speech precision with interpretation to musicality (Garnier et al., 2007).

Another important aspect of analysing these songs and performing French art songs is the phonetic change of French over the centuries. Since the French phonetic properties underwent many transformations, pronunciation norms emerged, affecting vocal interpretation. Understanding such shifts helps improve pronunciation accuracy and encourages performers to engage with the stylistic and cultural information embedded in various historical periods. This may allow singers to achieve historical authenticity in their performances by exploring phonetic variations popularised during Romanticism and Symbolism (Parker, 2015). Such insights emphasise the conversation between language and music that animates mélodies, letting phonetics become a window for venturing beyond the text-based page into culture and art.

This is especially true in the case of French phonetics, which is quite significant in respect to teaching. Languages: Modern vocal pedagogy embraces classical methods and new ideas and provides singers with guidance options for addressing the pitfalls of the deceptively subtle nature of French or whatever language the song prevails in when in a mélodie. Things like Richard Miller's The Structure of Singing and Adams' A Handbook for Diction, as well as online coaching platforms, have made phonetic training more available. This developmental pedagogy connects the need for well-rounded, vigilant performers responding to the demanding nuances of the French repertoire with the increasingly prominent role of phonetics (Adams, 2022).

This chapter examines the impact of pronunciation on the performance of mélodies, particularly its influence on articulation, resonance, historical context, and pedagogical concepts. By analysing and unpicking these components, the chapter aims to offer some insights for performers, teachers, and researchers on the language and artistry needed for the genre. As a vocalist and movement scientist, I believe integrating French phonetics in vocal training can enrich vocal precision and is the bridge between the mechanics of sound production and the interpretative potentialities offered in the classical music tradition.

Aim of the study

In this chapter, the study explores the intimacy of French phonetics and the performance of French art songs and how familiarity with these linguistic complexities leads to a clear and resonant singing voice, which has been integrated in the first sections through the act of singing. It also aims to discern functional pedagogical methods of teaching French phonetics to singers about traditional and contemporary approaches.

Research Questions

1. What specific phonetic challenges in French language pronunciation hinder the articulation of French art songs?
2. How does mastery of French phonetics affect vocal resonance and emotional expression in French mélodies?
3. How do historical shifts in French pronunciation influence the stylistic and cultural interpretation of French art songs?
4. What pedagogical methods are most effective in teaching French phonetics to vocalists?
5. How do the phonetic challenges of French compare with those found in other languages commonly used in classical vocal repertoire?

Research Objectives

1. To find the defining phonetic features of the French language that challenge singers in articulating art songs.
2. To examine the impact of ability in French phonetics on vocal resonance and emotional expressiveness.
3. To investigate the role of historical phonetic shifts in shaping the stylistic and cultural interpretation of French art songs.
4. To evaluate pedagogical approaches that effectively address the challenges of teaching French phonetics to singers.
5. To compare the phonetic challenges of French with those of other languages in the classical vocal repertoire.

6. To assess how phonetic mastery enhances French art song performances' authenticity and interpretative depth.

Significance of the study

This chapter explores the prosperous relationship between phonetics and vocal artistry as informed by the stated research questions and purpose. This chapter provides theoretical and practical contributions to the academic literature on voice performance and pedagogy in its approach to these issues. It concludes that scrutinising French phonetics is not merely a matter of technical correctness but encourages singers and educators to explore the cultural, historical and emotional layers behind mélodies. Thereby harnessing the sonic energy of the lyric and shaping their performance to reflect the emotional state of both the character and the more remarkable musical narrative, performers achieve greater authenticity (undoubtedly a goal of many artists) and create moving performances that resonate on a level rare to vocal only performance due, of course, to the skills of phonetic precision.

Literature Review

Pronunciation is a basic yet detailed study area for all musicians, especially in French art songs. French mélodies are distinctive for their complex poetic text and musical expression interrelationships. Due to the French language's phonetic features, singers looking for linguistic clarity, vocal resonance and emotion meet specific challenges. Phonetic accuracy for performing these songs is discussed throughout the literature as key to the performance of this genre.

The present article reviews research on the salient phonetic properties defining French, the influence of phonetic precision on the resonance of the phonatory apparatus, the repercussions of phonemic mergers that have occurred over the history of the French language on correct articulation, and pedagogical considerations resulting from these observations. It focuses on gathering information from three relevant subjects, phonetics, vocal pedagogy and music history, to parse French idiomatic pronunciation's influence on the mélodie repertoire. It also examines the relationship of French phonetics to other languages, giving context for the ingenuity needed to navigate the idiosyncrasies that make the French language particularly difficult for singers in classical vocal traditions.

In the literature, the lack of historical phonetic studies applied to vocal training is noted, along with the necessity for creative pedagogical solutions to the difficulties of French diction. This is a foundation of understanding how singers negotiate those barriers to present performances that require technical prowess and emotional conveyance. The intricacy of French diction is particularly weighty regarding the interpretation of music in art song form, for the phonetic features and linguistic subtleties can all change the interpretive phrasing of the music. French is about phonetic precision, intonation, and the cultural resonances that carry in pronunciation. This demands that a singer must juggle musical and emotional expression with the intricacies of the language itself (Miller, 2002; Fontaine, 2020).

Vowel Articulation and Its Impact on Vocal Timbre

When singing in a foreign language, even if it is something as rich and complex as French, thanks to the songs of artists like Édith Piaf, being able to pronounce and master the articulation handed down through generations in the vowel sounds is key. French phonology features distinctions between closed vowels (such as [i]) and open ones (like [ɑ] and [ɛ]), requiring different positions for the tongue and lip. These nuances alter the clarity of pronunciation and vocal resonance. For example, the French [ɑ], articulated with a lowered jaw and retracted tongue, requires careful breath control and resonant modulation to produce a warm, rich sound (Garnier et al., 2007).

It is vowels, not consonants, are the basis of vocal resonance. 'Vowel' execution helps singers achieve a more emotive and impactful performance. As Davids and La Tour (2012) note, we can significantly develop diction and range via vowel production, allowing performers to better convey the text's emotionally charged intention. The shaping of vowels is necessary for clarity, vocal color, and resonance to add beauty and richness to the performance.

Also, proper vowel formation governs the breath and air, vital to keeping vocal tone. Doing this correctly will allow effective use of breath so that the vocal folds are not strained and the area between notes, and even long phrases, will be much smoother. One such feature that seems to be compromised is the formation of the vowel space, ultimately resulting in decreased loudness and clarity of the voice (Reetz & Jongman, 2020). So, singers must learn to use a fine ear for tiny differences in vowels, breathe deeply without an expansive movement that would cause the soft palate to drop, and alter the mouth's shutter shape to try to elicit resonance but also not tire the voice. French holds nasal vowels, which add a dimension of difficulty for non-native speakers and singers. This gives nasal vowels such as [ã] in "sans" and [ɔ̃] in "nom" their distinctive sound, but to do this correctly, you need to control the soft palate. Producing these sounds (through air passing through the nose) is especially tricky for singers accustomed to more straightforward vowel production (like English). Nasal vowels demand a specific technique whereby singers must optimise the balance between resonance and air pressure, thus making articulating such vowels without impairing voice clarity or sound quality an indispensable technique (Machaney, 2006).

Clarke (2021) highlights the importance of clear nasal vowel articulation in achieving a natural-sounding French vocal tone, essential for performing French art songs. Academically trained singers often excel in managing nasal resonance, a critical skill for authentic French diction (Nemes, 2022). Sliding or fluttering the vocal folds can enhance nasalised vowel clarity (Doremus & Becker, 2022). However, Devedas, Kumar and Maruthy (2020) discovered that improper articulation can lead to excessive tension in the vocal folds, negatively affecting vocal technique and endurance. This underscores the need for precise training in nasal vowel production to support vocal health and sustain high-level performance.

Moreover, nasal vowels are important for emotional expressiveness in French art songs. They are often nasal vowels, and their correct use adds emotional heft to the performance, words that suggest longing or sadness. According to Fontaine (2020), nasal vowels in French lyrics are historically important from a phonetics point of view and mastering nasal vowels grants singers authentic performances of French songs. The nasal quality of French vowels could help explain why emotional nuances, whether longing, melancholy or romantic desire, can loom much more significant in French songs than in pop [exaggeration] English songs; you do not need to know the translation because the words become sounds and sound a melody. Fontaine (2020) argues that nasal vowels express an emotional nuance in the lyric, allowing a singer to embody the text (and its delivery). However, improper articulation of nasal vowels can lead to excessive strain and fatigue of the voice, diminishing the performance's emotionality (Machaney, 2006). In addition, improper nasal resonance can hinder the clarity and balance of the singer's overall sound, thus creating vocal fatigue.

The importance of consonant sounds in French art songs and emotional conveyance

In vocal training, vowels tend to be the focus as they are the most produced from the mouth. However, consonants change just as much of a piece's emotional quality. In French, consonants, the guttural "r" like a stiff joke (ʁ), and the spare "l" make a significant mark on articulation and vocal quality. The French "r," made at the back of the throat, can be especially tricky for singers not used to making this sound. A nasty, over-accelerated "r" can give a checked, rasping character, quickly robbing the idiom of a supportive resonance (Miller, 1999). However, appropriately phrased, it waxes fluidity and smoothness into any vocal line, mainly in legato phrasing.

However, things like the "r" and "l" are consonants that also affect things like the rhythm of a song and how expressive it is. They guarantee clarity and improve phrasing and flow when pronounced. Sing is taught to care for the consonant to enrich the melodic line and complete the interpretation. The importance of balancing the tone with technical correctness with emotive consonants in a vocal performance cannot be exaggerated (Ngobeni, Mukenge, Mpetshwa, 2024). In French, the "r," often produced at the back of the throat, presents a particular challenge to non-native singers. However, it can bring a unique texture to the vocal performance (Miller, 1999). For instance, as Ngobeni, Mukenge, and Mpetshwa (2024) point out, consonants are mastered, including challenging sounds such as the "r", to reach an equilibrium between technical proficiency and emotive expression. Likewise, the French "l" should be pronounced precisely, avoiding allowing the voice to turn either overly breathy or harsh, keeping even the surrounding phrases in the song in smooth stitch."

Also, consonants affect the total resonance of the voice. French consonants add clarity and projection to the sound when they occur, especially at the start or the end of a phrase. When consonants are not articulated crisply, they can weaken the tone of the voice while reducing volume and quality. Based upon their findings, Hisch, Pauseweng-Gelfer, and Booinin (2019) state that the development of consonant articulation-improving exercises needs to be incorporated into vocal training as it will change their resonation quality, thus preventing the development of vocal strain to ensure that the emotional semantics of vocalisation.

Linguistic Changes Over Time in the French Phonetic System: How Are They Useful for Singers?

The pronunciation of French has changed throughout history, and some historical phonetic shifts persist in the way we sing the language today. For example, in older French, certain vowels had alternative pronunciations. This is important for singers performing French art songs. Ervelius (2019) notes such changes, such as loss of word-final consonants in some words, noting that singers and choirs need to align their diction with the phonetics at the time of the song. Such shifts can not only change the sound but can also shift the emotional heft of the music, with different pronunciations carrying possibly different cultural or historical evocations.

Such historical phonetic shifts are crucial for a performer to bear in mind if the goal is to authentically bring to life the repertoire of the French art song. Singers can learn the phonetic features and aspects of earlier performances by learning aspects of older tapes, etc. In recent years, an increasing focus on historically informed performance has prompted scholars and performers to understand pronunciation to signal emotional and cultural frames endemic to a piece (Bergeron, 2010; Adams, 2022). To illustrate, earlier French art songs might have more rounded vowels, which then developed into a more closed sound. However, singers must also learn to adjust to these things to keep the song's integrity. Understanding these changes to French pronunciation, most notably the transition from more open vowels to closed sounds, is key to a historically informed performance. Singers must consider these historical subtleties to effectively sing the pieces (Ervelius, 2019; Adams, 2022). This understanding enables performers to draw from the song's historical and emotional context as they reflect its original stylistic and linguistic attributes. "Consulting old recordings and primary texts allows modern singers to get as close to a phonetic style of earlier periods as possible, which means they are performing with a sense of the piece's original cultural and emotional intents."

Moreover, knowledge of the phonetic shifts in French over history also helps singers understand how songs have evolved. For example, there are differences between French songs from the Baroque and Classical periods and those from the Romantic period in articulating vowels and consonants. By studying the historical and social context of the songs, singers can implement vocal techniques that they know are appropriate to the stylistic and linguistic properties of the period, deepening their connection to French vocal tradition.

Innovative Teaching Methods of French Phonetics in Singing

Recent advances in vocal pedagogy use technology to support singers through the complexities of French phonetics. Online resources like the International French Diction School provide interactive exercises that allow singers to hear and replicate proper pronunciation: a connection between phonetic theory and vocal practice. As Boudin (2020) observes, these digital resources are significant for singers with limited access to native-speaking coaches, enabling them to practice at their own pace to perfect their diction.

In this regard, traditional pedagogical approaches, like lip trills and diction drills, have mostly been concerned with physical elements of enunciation, helping singers accomplish the proper rounding and crispness of vowels and diphthongs. However, contemporary pedagogical techniques incorporate these approaches with technology, resulting in a more holistic training method. It gives singers the tools to learn the intricacies of the French phonetic system and incorporate this knowledge into their vocal technique, polishing their technical accuracy and emotional expressiveness. Mean Physical exercise has been implemented because certain pedagogical concealed ultimately relied on physical exercises, such as lip trills and diction drills, to round and sharpen the vowels and diphthongs. However, newer approaches are to blend these exercises with technology. Thanks to the emergence of online platforms such as the International French Diction School, singers can now use novel tools to independently train their French pronunciation, helping them perfect both their phonetic reproduction and singing (Boudin, 2020). These online tools help fill the void for singers who do not have immediate access to mentors in the French-speaking world by providing a more interactive, hip, and backstage way of learning.

Methodology

The current study takes a qualitative approach and features an extensive literature survey highlighting how French phonetics intersects with voice in performing French art songs. A qualitative method was employed to investigate the literature, theoretical constructs, and approaches to pedagogy related to French phonetics and vocal performance (Alder, 2002; Magiera, 2024). This approach aims to look for trends, themes, and key findings about the phenomenon of consonant precision in vocal technique and artistic expression in a sample of French art songs.

Data Collection

This study uses a literature review as the primary data collection method. The searches employed the following terms: "French phonetics in singing," "vocal articulation in French art songs," "French diction for singers," and "pedagogical approaches to teaching French phonetics." These terms were applied to extensive searches of multiple academic databases, including Google Scholar, JSTOR, ProQuest, and ResearchGate (Olarngbe, Sulyman & Aremu, 2024). In refining this search to find textual sources, the emphasis became on finding reliable texts that would elucidate the nuances of French phonetics as they pertain directly to the work of the voice, that of the classical and operatic traditions. The collection for this study aimed to prioritise articles from peer-reviewed journals and articles and books published in academic journals over the last 20 years, as an academic authority was established for the selected sources.

Eligibility Criteria

Specific inclusion and exclusion criteria were applied to the sources selected to ensure academic rigour. The study mainly reviewed sources on an explicit approach to French phonetics within vocal performance (Elliot, 2006). Such information made it possible to understand some of the phonetic subtleties singers have to control to sing French art songs successfully (Grau, 2016; Doyle, 2024). Publications on pedagogical methods for teaching French phonetics to singers also trumped. Sources focused on general linguistics or language acquisition, but not their use for musical application, were not included since these were outside the bounds of this study.

Thematic Analysis

Data were collected by analysing the identified sources to find relevant themes, findings and methodologies. These insights have been thematically analysed and tagged into key themes to explore, with focus areas including the connection between producing speech sounds accurately to the vibrations in the voice, the importance of producing high-fidelity French vowel and consonant sounds, and teaching and learning challenges for singers studying French phonetics. The analysis found several common themes, including:

Explore how vowel and consonant articulation and placement impact vocal resonance and clarity in this month's Technical Considerations in French Phonetics theme. The crisp articulation of French vowels, including nasalised ones, and consonants, particularly the guttural "r," is vital to the transparency and emotional expressiveness of the performance.

Vocal Resonance and Articulation

Research shows that articulation correlates directly with resonance. As Li (2018) explains, phonetic placement gives fullness and depth to vocal sounds. By grasping the phonetic patterns of French, singers can deliver more affluent, more vibrant, emotionally resonant performances.

Teaching Methods

According to the literature, efficient teaching practices of French phonetics often synthesise auditory practice and study visual feedback and kinaesthetic tasks. Explore these guides to implement linguistics in your work for best growth (Novotny, 2021; Henderson, 2021). Historical Phonetics of French: It explores the historical pronunciation shifts in French (Bybee, 2015; Crystal, 2018) and their effect on modern vocal performance. Therefore, for singers to accurately interpret these style shifts, the integrity of language and emotional weight attached to specific phonetics must remain intact, ideally whilst being linguistically prepared.

Theoretical Framework

The research method follows the principles of Self-Determination Theory (SDT) and Cognitive Load Theory (CLT). Self-determination theory (SDT) is a theory of motivation that focuses on fostering the educational environment to promote effective learning (Bailey, 2021; Pukli, 2022; Slemp, Field & Cho, 2020). When mastering French phonetics, these elements are essential for the singer's performance to be expressed precisely and expressively. Likewise, CLT points to the thinking demands of learning complex skills like the details of French diction. Knowing the cognitive load of mastering French phonetics can enable educators to create a pedagogy that does not waste cognitive resources and increases efficacy (Hubbel, 2019).

Methodology limitations

While the literature review method provides an excellent analysis of the existing body of knowledge, this method has certain limitations. One limitation concerns the breadth of available sources: certain publications may have gone unnoticed, particularly those in languages other than English or those that did not appear widely. Finally, the thematic analysis performed is subjective, and the interpretation of the data can still be influenced by personal bias, although transparency and objectivity were implemented. Moreover, being a study using only secondary sources, it does not provide primary data in findings of empirical studies or interviews with first-hand singers or vocal teachers, which could provide another perspective on the practical use of the theoretical results.

Limitations of the Study

However, while this study offers important insight into the effect of French phonetics on vocal performance, it does have its limitations. One major limitation is that it specialises only in French art songs. It includes phonemic challenges and musical articulation techniques that address the endless subtleties of French phonetics in this genre. These results may not generalise across other vocal repertoires. The phonetic difficulties experienced by singers singing in languages other than their native tongue, for example, Italian, German, or English, can vary greatly. Consequently, approaches to articulation by singers in these languages may differ from those utilised in this study, reducing the applicability of the results to non-classical vocal genres. Each language engenders a phonetic environment with its demands, requiring unique pedagogical approaches.

Another key limitation is that the study relied on literature and secondary sources for the data collection. Because the study is a literature review and does not present original data or direct observation of the phonetic mastery of singers, conclusions are drawn from documented tendencies and theories rather than first-hand encounters. This dependence limits the study's ability to review recent trends in pedagogical practices, particularly those involving modern methodologies and technological innovations. Lacking original empirical data- such as singers being interviewed or their voices assessed phonetically- the results are confined to interpretations of what is already out there, and they do not begin to address the many changes dynamically underway in vocal pedagogy.

Secondly, the study is primarily theoretical, discussing the most theoretical aspects of French Phonetics and providing a few practical examples of how theory is put into practice. As such, while this study delineates a theoretical framework, that framework does not necessarily prescribe real-world pedagogical frameworks because teaching methods, resources, and institutional structure can diverge significantly in varied educational settings. It may also ignore the difficulties that non-French speakers have when it comes to using the entire phonetic structure of the French language (in particular, the phoneme of French vs. foreign language). As a result, one important component of this phonetic training's potential impact on global speaker populations has yet to be thoroughly investigated.

In addition, no consideration of how these alternative approaches to phonetics training compare in their long-term effectiveness or their transferability to other aspects of singers' vocal technique and artistry is discussed. Although this study offers insight into current practices and pedagogical methods, it does not account for the lasting impact on singers from mastering French phonetics throughout their development. Future studies should examine the lasting effects of phonetic training, helping to clarify how this training serves as a foundational element of singers' technical and expressive development and adding to our knowledge of the effects of this phonetic mastery on vocal performance as a complete picture.

Finally, the study is a fascinating contribution to understanding how French phonetics presents challenges in vocal performance. Its limited scope (dealing only with French art songs), dependence on secondary sources, and absence of empirical evidence indicate the need for more research. A deeper working through of this topic beyond the perceived arcane (the understanding rests on the lives of those who lead), including the application to pedagogy and the evidentiary in an applied way, would make for more than an incomplete softening of complex behaviour to help vocal performance across several repertoires. This review highlights some shortcomings of current models and suggests future work to integrate a more realistic and applied model of French phonetic realities in singing.

Findings

French Phonetics and its Effect on Speech

The study underscored the significance of French phonetics in shaping the articulation of French art songs, focusing on the precise differentiation between closed vowels ([i]) and open vowels ([ɑ]). Those who had exercised their brains to distinguish between these subtle phonetic contrasts could better articulate their singing, which is necessary for language and plays a significant role in performing emotional expression. As shown in the study, this enunciation of vowels allows the meaning of the lyrics and their emotional radical to come through nicely, enhancing audience comprehension and involvement with the performance.

Indeed, as Wu (2020) mentions, the phonetic detail of French vowels is essential in realising French art songs, and every phonetic detail helps to deliver the emotion of that text. These singers, who understand little phonetic details, succeed even more in delivering the intensity contained in what is being sung. Such attention to detail in articulation helps singers forge their way through the subtleties of the French language and preserve and communicate the emotional qualities of the text.

However, singers who were less acquainted with French phonetics could not articulate the text with the same degree of focus. According to Badawi (2023), they did not enunciate and mispronounce vowels, resulting in distorted pronunciation and weakening their performance's emotional impact. Singers had trouble delivering an intelligible performance and maintaining an emotional presence, especially in phrases requiring precision of enunciation, including precise placement of vowels and adjacent consonants. The study details these challenges and how an understanding can enhance a well-resonating and impressive voice.

Sound Ornaments: Phonetic Versatility

One of the most salient themes in the study was the link between phonetic accuracy and the resonance of the voice in the French art song. The study cited principles in The Diction for Singers by Pierre Bernac (Grossberg, 2003), showing that attention to consonant articulation makes for a more resonant and expressive vocal sound among singers. Correct placement of hard consonants in complex properties that came as a bonus sonorities bottom out when the singer has no proper context or volume and can only produce all the guttural elements without the necessary synchronisation.

Crystal-clear enunciation of the consonants played a significant role in the dynamics and phrasing of the music. Singers who articulated their consonants clearly (a term some vocal pedagogues have used) could bend their vocal resonance, altering the sound according to the song's emotional needs. In dramatic passages, for example, clear consonant articulation heightened intensity and emotional expression.

The study revealed that singers who had perfected their French phonetics created a homogenous, resonant sound from the lower ranges to the higher demands of the vocal line. Such resonance is a direct consequence of phonetic training, essential to vocal performance in French art songs. Together, these findings highlight the importance of phonetic work less as an end but rather as a means of refining the singer's vocal imprint, enriching their sonic pallet and technical artistry so they can produce more expressive and nuanced performances.

Historical Phrasing Explanation

The study also examined earlier phonetic changes in French that have changed modern singers' renditions of French art songs. Moreover, the French language has evolved over the centuries, as has the singers' approach to the works (Apter, Herman, 2016; Potter, 2006). Singers who understood these historical changes could better grasp the stylistic and emotional framework in which certain pieces were written. By exploring phonetic diversity throughout history, singers can find an extra-historically informed approach to French art songs, recreating the phonetic media one might expect when the pieces were first composed. This brought greater authenticity and cultural context to their performance, providing a deeper emotional connection to the songs' historical significance.

Modern French art song interpreters, who had only encountered modern French when confronted with traditional French art songs, especially those with regional phonetic variants or gene assistant archaic pronunciations, became confused and unable to interpret and perform. Despite these vulnerabilities, singers who utilised historical phonetic variations received corresponding praise for their performances' greater depth, authenticity, and character. Research advances the importance of understanding historical and modern French phonetics in vocal training to cultivate more informed and culturally competent interpretations of French art songs.

To summarise, this study segment underscores the necessity of awareness of modern and ancient phonetic practices in vocal pedagogy. This comprehension enables clarion performances from linguistically bona fide singers and culturally ennobled. Learning how phonetics in French has evolved gives any singer a rabbit hole in how to be more time-period appropriate in making French sounds come out.

Pedagogical Impact on Phonetic Mastery

The study revealed that pedagogical methods were pivotal in singers' understanding of French phonetics. According to the research, well-structured teaching approaches with creative aspects contribute significantly to developing phonetic skills in singers. Inspired by Richard Miller's 1996 book On the Art of Singing, Fontaine's 2020 Diction in Context, and Adams's 2022 Diction for Singers, King's study illustrated that employing familiar, contemporary resources in the learning process improved students' mastery of French pronunciation significantly more efficiently than traditional methods. Notably, singers who used the information provided them with the International French Diction School, an online platform to improve phonetic accuracy, benefited the most, underlining the importance of technology in the future of vocal pedagogy.

Other standard techniques, like individual practice with a sequence of phonetic syllables and daily repetition, also continued to be important to the phonetic training of singers. The study found that those who received instruction concentrated on where to place a vowel, how to pronounce a consonant, and how to convey emotion in the text; they significantly improved their performance during expressiveness testing. At the same time, incorporating these components into their training made students learn them through French phonetics and better emphasise proper pronunciation's role in ensuring linguistically accurate and phonetically expressive performance.

Using technology to shape pedagogy, especially if using interactive platforms that give immediate feedback on pronunciation, enables students to find and target specific areas of difficulty more effectively. A data-driven combination of this focused feedback alongside traditional corrective methods made a remarkable difference in the proficient use of French sounds. The findings highlight the value of using old and new teaching tools in mastering French phonics. This integrated approach ensures linguistic precision and enhances expressive and emotionally resonant performances, a key factor in many global vocal traditions.

Phonetic Comparison of French

The study also cast light on the known difficulties singers encounter when studying French phonetics compared to other languages. French has challenges, notably with differentiating vowel and consonant sounds (Ivanova et al., 2018). The subtleties of French pronunciation, including nasal vowels and silent letters, require scrutiny from the singer, less so in other languages. Singers who were not well exposed to French or whose native language was quite different adjusted better than expected, which means they could transfer learning strategies from other languages to work out how to tackle the phonetic challenges posed by French.

Trubach, Gorshkova, and Sklyer (2023) presented research exploring the phonological elements of the French art song repertoire that increase understanding. Although you may encounter similar allophones in other languages, French offers unique challenges due to its many vowel distinctions or consonant clusters. It was clear from examples that singers who understood and could recreate these nuances reached a greater level of fluency and expressiveness in their singing, reinforcing the idea that a detailed understanding of French phonetics is necessary to interpret French art songs effectively.

This study also discussed the benefits of learning French phonetics through multilingualism (Kim & Lee, 2001). Singers fluent in multiple languages, especially Romance languages like Italian or Spanish, could use their prior knowledge of how phonetic sounds correspond in other languages to make the transition to French easier. Nevertheless, the study also noted that while Romance languages share many characteristics, this can lead to peculiarities in French due to its unique pronunciation rules. It is essential for everyone, from singers to singers of all languages, to focus on phonetic training.

Overall, the results highlight the need for a proper understanding and mastery of French phonetics for practical and beautiful renditions of this genre of vocal performance. Seekers of linguistic insight might find a multilingual approach helpful, particularly when singers adjust their pronunciations phonemically. However, most would ultimately need to be taught some aspect of the phonological system of French over time to perform at a high level.

Discussion

Understanding the Challenges of Articulation

By examining which French vowels prove difficult for singers in performing French art songs, the study's findings illuminate these challenges with articulating French vowels. The difference between [i] and [ɑ], closely related sounds (where [ɑ] is an open sound and [i] is closed), exemplifies the challenges singers face deciphering the webs of French phonetics. This contrast in vowel sounds makes a notable difference in how the lyrics come across and how much sentiment the words carry (Demirezen, 2023). Singers, moreover, must find a balance between being phonetically accurate and conveying the emotional content of a song so that they enunciate clearly while performing with power.

Phonetic Accuracy and Emotional Expression in French Art Song

Performance For singers with difficulty with vowel articulation, this also posed the danger of detracting from their immersion in the emotional depth of the lyrics. The mispronunciations took the chance of muddying the words' meaning, resulting in emotionally broad performances. However, singers who could master vowel articulation could use it to improve their lyrical expression and heighten the emotional effect of the song. Thus, phonetic training is still a cornerstone of vocal pedagogy, allowing the performer to excel in linguistic accuracy and emotional delivery.

Moreover, the study underscores the crucial role of vocal instructors in guiding singers through these articulatory difficulties. Vowel actions governed by musical intonation considerations (they are not here) and pedagogical approaches for proper production of them (especially for the dramatic narrative style that runs through all the French art songs) are priceless. Unfortunately, without adequate training and instruction, singers may not know how to manage these nuances and may lose some of the meaning or intention of the song. It argues for an organised pedagogy of French diction encompassing phonetic precision and expressive musicality, merging technical skills with the emotional content that singers must feel comfortable embedding in their work.

How Phonetics and Resonance are Woven Together

Data collected from study subjects showed a robust correlation between the accuracy of a subject's phonetic articulation and the resonance of their voice. This finding underlines the importance of proper articulation to produce a well-rounded sound. Based on Bernac's tenets of diction (Kudina & Coeckelbergh, 2021), the study concluded that singers with high phonetic accuracy, especially concerning consonant sounds, were able to create a richer, more resonant vocal sound. The relationship between phonetics and resonance shows us that phonetic mastery, notably the French way of pronouncing phonemes, directly affects the intelligibility and acoustic quality of the singer's voice. Consonants make words come alive; careful use of consonants shows more definition in vocal performance so that the subtleties of lyric phrasing, dynamics, etc., are conveyed.

The study will have broader relevance for any singer who performs in different tongues, highlighting the power of phonetic training. Although this study was conducted on French art songs, phonetic accuracy and resonance principles can be applied to all vocal music. Dictation improves articulation and vowel production and aids voice health and sound production. This overview highlights the importance of considering phonetics as a vital aspect of vocal pedagogy for linguistic intelligibility and developing an animated, resonant voice model. Singers with excellent phonetic control can create a deep, sonorous, expressive sound that carries well in a concert hall.

Exploring Historical Phonetics as a Doorway to Cultural Expression

Exploring the evolution of phonetic shifts in the historical development of the French vocal tradition underlines the need for musicians working with French art songs to be aware of the gradual shaping of the pronunciation of French. By adopting certain historical phonetic variations, singers could effectively channel the linguistic traits that defined a given era, imbuing their act with cultural authenticity. This draws on Macy's work with the vocal practices of Eckert and Labou (2017), which shows how a tightened nexus can occur between historical phonetics and everyday cultural expression. Exploring phonetic changes throughout history allows singers to give a more authentic interpretation of French art songs, which harkens to the cultural and historical context in which these works.

The study also complements the changing nature of language and its effect on music. As French pronunciation has evolved through the years, so has the way singers navigate French art songs. When singers understand this and the recognisably modern sound of English, they can interpret songs with more depth and accuracy, ensuring their performances remain faithful to the music's original cultural context and its modern-day interpretation. Singers, therefore, act as curators of cultural propagation, keeping linguistic subtleties that allow for the continued development of French vocal music.

Nonetheless, the conversation also recognises the difficulties of integrating historical phonetic variance into performance practice, which can be especially problematic for singers trained in modern French pronunciation. Engaging older phonetic standards involves a deep musical understanding of the song's historical moment and a looser grip on pronunciation. Including historical phonetics may be challenging, but it ultimately leads to a performance with many more shades of meaning and representative of the culture.

Lastly, the conversation highlights historical phonetics' important role in performing French art songs. Embracing historical pronunciation evolutions can help singers present more authentic and culturally rich renditions of musical works, giving the audience a more profound sense of the origins of the music while simultaneously keeping it alive and relevant in the present. This preserves cultural traditions and adds an interpretive depth to the music so that French art songs may resonate with audiences throughout time.

Where pedagogy and policymaking are unanticipated

This study offers minimum pedagogical guidance on potential phonetic development templates and techniques for modern singers (Beknozarova, 2024). The results confirmed existing correlations between current trends in vocal pedagogy, which combine traditional methods with contemporary technology, and the law of the rigidity of the classic "lesson" that singers face while learning French phonetics. These challenges significantly depart from the traditional outcomes models (Bertrand, 2022). In teaching the phonetics of any vocal subjects, nothing was so interactive and engaging for students as today with digital means in classrooms combined with online teaching (up to October 2023).

However, the conversation also underscored the enduring value of classic teaching methods, including personalised instruction and tailored feedback. Integrating classical methods with modern technology enables educators to help singers clarify their diction more effectively. Consistent with its findings, meaning-based learning is proposed as a future goal for combining traditional and contemporary learning methods to provide a complete education for singers.

It enables teachers of French learners to discover new methods of instructing French phonetics. It draws particular attention to the challenges posed by the intricacies of the French phonemic system and the expectations for expressive, authentic performances while asserting that educators must equip singers to face this challenge (Cashman, 2019). The study recommends a hybrid solution by combining modern technological tools and pedagogical practices so that vocal pedagogy can grow to support the needs of modern-day singers. This approach not only helps the singers master the nuts and bolts of French phonetics but also allows them to express themselves artistically and emotionally. Pedagogical methods discussed in the literature depend on an adaptable teaching philosophy that responds to rapid developments in knowledge and pedagogy." This helps singers attain a thorough technical command of French phonetics and expressive and inflected singing.

The Multilingual Challenge on How to Navigate

Compared with other languages, the study of French phonetics highlights the challenges that singers face when singing French art songs (Miller, 1996). French art songs are challenging to understand due to their unique phonetic characteristics and vowel pronunciation. This study shows that these phonetic subtleties are more often a challenge than an obstacle, but they also make the interpretation of French music so evocative and poignant.

Singers are almost always expected to be able to match the nuances of French vowel sounds, which can be quite different from those in other languages. Although this makes finding the correct resonance and clarity of sound more treacherous, they are fundamental to providing a genuine performance. This challenge is further magnified when singers sing in a language that is not their first language. So, familiarising oneself with phonetics is as important as the precision of the voice to add the emotional scale, where not just the lyrical weight but the cultural understanding of the music lives.

Understanding these phonetic challenges can help voice teachers provide specific strategies to guide singers through the intricacies of French speech. This study proposes a pedagogy that prioritises meticulous pronunciation of the French vowel system's phonemes and encourages singers to interpret the technical aspects of phonetic articulation and openness collaboratively. However, story-rich sonic landscapes are present in French art songs to build the emotional narrative. Finding the balance between precision and expression opens singers to the language, recasting what might feel like a technical pitfall as an expressive mechanism that adds to the performance.

Recommendations

The Importance of Phonetic Instruction in Vocal Programs

Phonetic learning is integral to building one's practical singing skills in a French context. These structured lessons concentrate on articulation and resonance and are central to building a strong foundation for singers. These lessons connect classroom theory and application and allow students to internalise the nuances of French vowels and consonants. Native French coaches and linguists may collaborate with students to enhance their learning experience about technical knowledge and the nuances of the language.

An example: How to use tech for phonetic practice

One practical application of technology in phonetic practice involves using interactive language applications or speech analysis software. These tools provide real-time feedback, helping singers improve their articulation, vowel production, and phonetic accuracy in languages like French. Technological advancements and artificial intelligence provide opportunities for enhancing phonetic application. Interactive software with real-time feedback is instrumental in helping singers refine their pronunciation and finding and correcting phonetic errors. Nasal vowels are an example of complex sounds that could benefit from audiovisual representations as tools to produce accurate phonetic sounds so that singers can align their scientific theoretic phonetic models with their actual voiced sounds in production. These tools can be harnessed and integrated into vocal programs, leading students through a customised, interactive learning process.

Discuss the French phonetic evolution through History

Beyond mastering French phonetics, one must understand its historical evolution. Examining vowel changes over centuries provides fresh interpretive possibilities for French art songs and aligns singers with the cultural and stylistic constellations that shape the medium. Shaping emotional content: Pronunciation plays a massive part in the technical accuracy of singing, and singers who study how pronunciation has been formulated can enhance their emotional content. Workshops based around these phonetic changes can also deepen singers' appreciation of the cultural contexts in which these works were written.

Talking to Native French Speakers One on One

Having native French speakers to learn from makes a tremendous difference to your French phonetic development. Masterclasses or workshops by native speakers or vocalists allow students to see how authentic pronunciation they have learned is realised in practice. These immersive sessions create an active environment where students can learn through constructive feedback and gain confidence. Breaking through phonetic barriers is precisely what this interaction helps, allowing students to hone themselves technically and expressively.

Access to quality resources

Phonetic training is an important study area, but limited resources are available. Such works as Richard Miller's On the Art of Singing and Alenzi (2024) provide vital insights into French phonetics. Along with online tutorials or video demonstrations, these resources provide alternative practices to learning. Institutions are better served by focusing on providing these materials to students, who can now study independently along with their structured time. This process allows students to understand further and develop their French phonetic skills.

Applicable teaching techniques like Personalized and Collaborative Learning

Programs must cater to the unique needs of non-native speakers, which can be sharply defined by the most arduous aspects of French phonetics, including silent letters and nasal vowels. Tailored exercises addressing these challenges can significantly enhance a student's skills. Including collaborative activities, such as group rehearsals and peer feedback sessions, helps students learn from one another, reinforcing their experiences while building a supportive network for growth through their shared learning (Westlund & Gaunt, 2023).

Exploratory Studies and New Directions for Pedagogy

Such investigation into sound pedagogy is ongoing and must be done to maintain a relevant and effective training program (Reflinda, Roza & Firdaus, 2024). Technology and developments are changing daily, which means that curricula need to be updated all the time. This empowers phonetic mastery by keeping the teaching style updated and relevant to the latest trends. Integration of feedback from both teachers and learners will also fine-tune training programs to the changing needs of singers.

Bridging the divide Between Technical Skill and Creative Expression

The recommendations also address a disconnection between technical skills and artistry (Huron, 2016; Rayan, 2020). A unified perspective of phonetic training technically and emotionally makes it possible for singers to rise to the technical challenges of French art songs. With a solid understanding of French phonetics and its musical application, singers can achieve technical precision alongside artistic expression, inviting fuller artistic potential.

Conclusion

This research offers new insights into engagement with French phonetics about vocal performance, especially when performing French art songs. This study explores challenges and strategies for specificity and expressiveness by examining the relationships between French vowels and articulation, phonetics and vocal resonance, how historical time has determined the evolution of French phonetics, and implications for teaching those complexities.

The research emphasises the need to transcend French phonetic barriers, considering specifically how such vowels and consonants shape vocal clarity, resonance, and emotional transmission. When singers master these phonetic hurdles, they create sharper diction and greater resonance and build a better link to the cultural and emotional narrative that the music demands. The final section examines the importance of understanding French historically to the singer's art and, more generally, the singer's ability to touch on the linguistic and cultural richness of the repertoire.

Moreover, this study highlights the importance of integrating classic and modern techniques to teach phonetics. Everyone can benefit from a hybrid approach of traditional teaching methods (auditory, video and desktop guides) mixed with contemporary aids (e.g. online resources and interactive diction exercises) to achieve higher fluency in French phonetics. In short, this study urges teachers to use a more à la carte, task-based, or contemporary skills-based approach to teach linguistic and artistic fluency, sensing that an increased understanding of French poetic guidelines will yield convincing deliveries of art song meanings.

Moreover, this research provides insights into the challenges of singers learning to sing in many languages. French phonetics are quite idiosyncratic compared to many other languages (in English, too, but you need more specificity when trying to understand French phonetics). Thus, singers who can adjust to the way French phonetics works can express the true nuances of the vocal music and bring their performances to a new level.

Although this investigation has contributed significantly to our understanding of vocal performance and diction, it has clear limitations. The results may not extend to other genres or languages and could be most pertinent to French art songs. Future studies might also examine how French pronunciation hurdles measure up to those posed by other languages or how singers from varied languages navigate the challenges of French diction.

Therefore, this study highlights the importance of employing phonetics at a deeper level for French art song performers to sing with vocal excellence and emotional integrity. It proposes a pedagogy combining classic methodologies with contemporary voicing innovations in service of singers, overcoming the challenges inherent in French phonetics and realising the fullness of artistic opportunity in the repertoire.

References

1. Adams, D. (2022). A Handbook of Diction for Singers. https://doi.org/10.1093/oso/9780197639504.001.0001
2. Alder, W. G. (2002). The acquisition of French phonology by adult anglophone learners: perceptions and realities, theory and practice (Doctoral dissertation, University of Southampton).
3. Alenezi, M. (2024). The French Influence on Modern English Orthography A Historical and Linguistic Analysis. Journal of Intercultural Communication, 183–190.LOCKSS.https://doi.org/10.36923/jicc.v24i4.914
4. Apter, R., & Herman, M. (2016). Translating for singing: The theory, art and craft of translating lyrics. Bloomsbury publishing.
5. Badawi, W. S. (2023). The French Phonetic Impact on English. JOURNAL OF LANGUAGE STUDIES, 6(3, 2), 14–30. https://doi.org/10.25130/jls.6.3.2.2
6. Bailey, E. N. (2021). University music ensemble participation and psychological well-being. The University of Utah. Beddor, P. S. (2023). Advancements of phonetics in the 21st century: Theoretical and empirical issues in the phonetics of sound change. Journal of Phonetics, 98,101228.https://doi.org/10.1016/j.wocn.2023.101228
7. Bradford, Z. (2019). Vocal resonance: Optimising source-filter interactions in voice training. Fusion Journal, (15), 47-70.
8. Beknazarova, T., Yussupova, A., Daurbayeva, G., Blagodarnaya, S., Smolianina, E., & Baigutov, K. (2024). Unravelling the Tapestry of Vocal Artistry: Navigating the Realm of Opera, Vocal Schooling, and Chamber Singing while Tracing the Evolution of Vocal Technique in Arias. Kurdish Studies, 12(2), 2431-2442.
9. Bertrand, M. (2022). Vocal Pedagogy in the Choral Rehearsal: A Multiple Case Study. Western Illinois University.
10. Cashman, P. V. (2019). International best practice teaching lyric diction to Conservatorium-level singers (Doctoral dissertation).
11. Castleberry, A., & Nolen, A. (2018). Thematic analysis of qualitative research data: Is it as easy as it sounds? Currents in Pharmacy Teaching and Learning, 10(6),807–815.https://doi.org/10.1016/j.cptl.2018.03.019
12. Christiner, M. (2020). Musicality and Second Language Acquisition: Singing and Phonetic Language. Aptitude (Doctoral dissertation, Dissertation, University of Vienna, Vienna, Austria).
13. Clarke, L. (2021). Vocal Synthetics: Designing for an Adaptable Singing Synthesizer (Doctoral dissertation, OCAD University).
14. Colapinto, J. (2021). This is the Voice. Simon and Schuster.

15. Crystal, D. (2018). The language revolution. John Wiley & Sons.

16. Delvaux, V., & Pillot-Loiseau, C. (2020). Perceptual Judgment of Voice Quality in Nondysphonic French Speakers: Effect of Task-, Speaker- and Listener-Related Variables. Journal of Voice, 34(5), 682–693. https://doi.org/10.1016/j.jvoice.2019.02.013

17. Derry, S. (2020). Diction in Context: Singing in English, Italian, German, and French, First Edition. Voice and Speech Review, 15(2), 241–243. https://doi.org/10.1080/23268263.2020.1827533

18. Devadas, U., Kumar, P. C., & Maruthy, S. (2020). Prevalence of and Risk Factors for Self-Reported Voice Problems Among Carnatic Singers. Journal of Voice, 34(2), 303.e1-303.e15. https://doi.org/10.1016/j.jvoice.2018.09.013

19. Doremus, S., & Becker, L. (2022). Improve Speech, Influence, and Connection With Others by Developing Your Professional Voice. Maximizing Your Communication Opportunities. https://doi.org/10.4135/9781071896006

20. Doyle, O. (2024). Beyond the Courtier: Music and Lifestyle Literature in Italy, 1480– 1530 (Doctoral dissertation, University of Sheffield)

21. Eckert, P., & Labov, W. (2017). Phonetics, phonology and social meaning. Journal of Sociolinguistics, 21(4), 467–496. Portico. https://doi.org/10.1111/josl.12244

22. Elliott, M. (2006). Singing in style: A guide to vocal performance practices. Yale University Press.

23. Garnier, M., Bernardoni, N. H., Castellengo, Sotiropoulos, D., & Dubois, D. (2007). Characterisation of voice quality in Western lyrical singing: From Teachers' judgements to acoustic descriptions. Journal of Interdisciplinary Music Studies, 1(2), 62-91.

24. Grau, A. K. (2010). Representation and Resistance: Female vocality in thirteenth-Century France (Doctoral dissertation, University of Pennsylvania).

25. Grossberg, S. (2003). Resonant neural dynamics of speech perception. Journal of Phonetics, 31(3–4), 423–445. https://doi.org/10.1016/s0095-4470(03)000512

26. Henderson, A. (2021). Intelligibility and identity: From teaching pronunciation to training for spoken language variation (Doctoral dissertation, Université Savoie Mont Blanc).

27. Hubbell, M. (2019). Early Twentieth Century Vocal Performance Practice and the French School: An Exploration of the Lectures and Selected Songs by Reynaldo Hahn (Doctoral dissertation, City University of New York).

28. Huron, D. (2016). Voice Leading. https://doi.org/10.7551/mitpress/9780262034852.001.0001

29. Hsia, L., & Hwang, G. (2020). Enhancing students' choreography and reflection in university dance courses: A mobile technology-assisted peer assessment

Approach. British Journal of Educational Technology, 52(1), 266–287. Portico.https://doi.org/10.1111/bjet.12986

30. Ivanova, I. G., Egoshina, R. A., Bazhenova, N. G., & Rusinova, N. V. (2018). On the importance of comparative phonetic analysis for bilingual language Learning. Issues and Trends in Interdisciplinary Behavior and Social Science, 219–224.https://doi.org/10.1201/9781315148700-32

31. Job, L. Y. F. C. (2013). 2013 ACDA NATIONAL CONFERENCE.

32. Kim, S. J., & Lee, E. Y. (2001). A Comparative Study of Korean and French Vowel Systems Experimental Phonetic and Phonological Perspective. Speech sciences, 8(1), 53-66.

33. Kudina, O., & Coeckelbergh, M. (2021). "Alexa, define empowerment": voice. Assistants at home, appropriation and techno performances. Journal of Information, Communication and Ethics in Society, 19(2), 299–312. https://doi.org/10.1108/jices-06-2020-0072

34. Lehrer, M. (2023). Challenges European EFL teachers face in pronunciation Teaching (Doctoral dissertation, University of Illinois at Urbana-Champaign).

35. Li, C. Y. (2018). Diction for Mandarin/Chinese Singers: A Methodology to Achieve Resonant Tone and Vowel Unification in Western Choral Music (Doctoral dissertation, University of South Carolina).

36. Mabry, S. (2002). Exploring Twentieth-Century Vocal Music. https://doi.org/10.1093/oso/9780195141986.001.0001

37. Macy, L. W. (Ed.). (2008). The Grove Book of Opera Singers. Oxford University Press.

38. Mahaney, C. L. (2006). Diction for singers: a comprehensive assessment of books And sources. The Ohio State University.

39. Magiera, R. (2024). Teaching Pronunciation and Intonation to Adults in Foreign Languages: A Qualitative Case Study (Doctoral dissertation, American College of Education).

40. Merlino, S. (2014). Singing in "another" language: how pronunciation matters in The organisation of choral rehearsals. Social Semiotics, 24(4), 420–445. https://doi.org/10.1080/10350330.2014.929390

41. Miller, R. (1999). Singing Schumann. https://doi.org/10.1093/oso/9780195119046.001.0001

42. Miller, R. (1996). Diction and Vocal Technique. On the Art of Singing, p. 26– https://doi.org/10.1093/acprof:osobl/9780195098259.003.0006

43. Miller, R. (1996). On the Art of Singing. https://doi.org/10.1093/acprof:osobl/9780195098259.001.0001

44. Miller, R. (2004). Solutions For Singers. https://doi.org/10.1093/oso/9780195160055.001.0001

45.Novotny, M. L. (2021). A system for high-variability training of French vowels: A design-based study (Master's thesis, Iowa State University).

46.Nemes, L. (2024). Rehearsal Techniques for Contemporary Choral Music. Perspectives on Conducting, 169–183. https://doi.org/10.4324/9781003299660-18

47.Olarongbe, S. A., Sulyman, A. S., Aremu, B. A., Balogun, B., & Suleiman, A. I. (2024). AWARENESS AND UTILIZATION OF ACADEMIC DATABASES AMONG LECTURERS OF KWARA STATE POLYTECHNIC, ILORIN, NIGERIA. A Journal of NLA IT Section Vol, 4, 1.

48.Parker, T. (2015). Tasting French Terroir. https://doi.org/10.1525/california/9780520277502.001.0001

49.Pukli, M. (2022). 55| 2022 Pronunciation Matters. Presses universitaires de Strasbourg.

50.Rambeau, A., & Koschwitz, E. (1894). French Phonetics. Modern Language Notes, 9(5), 138. https://doi.org/10.2307/2918219

51.Ragan, K. (2020). A systematic approach to voice: The art of studio application. Plural Publishing.

52.Reflinda, R., Roza, V., & Firdaus, F. (2024). Exploring Emerging Trends in Phonetics: The Influence of Orthographic Forms and Technological Integration in Language Learning. REiLA: Journal of Research and Innovation in Language, 6(2), 193-206

53.Reetz, H. and Jongman, A., (2020). Phonetics: Transcription, production, Acoustics and perception. John Wiley & Sons.

54.Slemp, G. R., Field, J. G., & Cho, A. S. H. (2020). A meta-analysis of autonomous And controlled forms of teacher motivation. Journal of Vocational Behavior, 121,103459.https://doi.org/10.1016/j.jvb.2020.103459

55.Spence, L. J. (2020). Preserving the Narrative of 20th Century Art Song: A Guide for Instrumental Transcriptions of Vocal Music (Doctoral dissertation, University of Maryland, College Park).

56.Tanjung S, A., Tobing, R. L., & Gultom, A. M. (2024). Analysis of French Orthographic Errors Among Students at a Vocational School in Yogyakarta. Formosa Journal of Sustainable Research, 3(8), 1689–1702. https://doi.org/10.55927/fjsr.v3i8.10999

57.Trubach, O. K., Gorshkova, D. I., & Sklyar, L. N. (2023). Comparative Analysis Of Phonetic Systems of the Russian, French and Chinese Languages. RUDN Journal of Language Studies, Semiotics and Semantics, 14(1), 171–188. https://doi.org/10.22363/2313-2299-2023-14-1-171-188

58.UEDA, H., & NIIYAMA, Y. (2019). Articulating Challenges in Defining Japanese Washoku and French Gastronomy. Journal of Food System Research, 26(3),144–164.https://doi.org/10.5874/jfsr.26.3_144

59.Weiss, M. J., Scrivener, S., Slaughter, A., & Cohen, B. (2021). An On-Ramp to Student Success: A Randomized Controlled Trial Evaluation of a Developmental Education Reform at the City University of New York. Educational Evaluation and Policy Analysis, 43(4), 555–586. https://doi.org/10.3102/01623737211008901

60.Wu, K. (2019). Difficulties for Chinese Vocalists in Singing French Art Song. Arizona State University.

www.ingramcontent.com/pod-product-compliance
Lightning Source LLC
Chambersburg PA
CBHW051336150726
47997CB00004B/1491